D1316230

PROMISES & PRAYERS

for Friends

FAMILY CHRISTIAN PRESS

PROMISES & PRAYERS

for Friends

FAMILY CHRISTIAN PRESS
Grand Rapids, MI 49530

ISBN 1-58334-133-1

The quoted ideas expressed in this book (but not scripture verses) are not, in all cases, exact quotations, as some have been edited for clarity and brevity. In all cases, the author has attempted to maintain the speaker's original intent. In some cases, quoted material for this book was obtained from secondary sources, primarily print media. While every effort was made to ensure the accuracy of these sources, the accuracy cannot be guaranteed. For additions, deletions, corrections or clarifications in future editions of this text, please write FAMILY CHRISTIAN PRESS.

Certain elements of this text, including quotations, stories, and selected groupings of Bible verses, have appeared, in part or in whole, in publications produced by Brighton Books of Nashville, TN; these excerpts are used with permission.

Printed in the United States of America
Cover Design & Page Layout: *Bart Dawson*

1 2 3 4 5 6 7 8 9 10 • 02 03 04 05 06 07 08 09 10

For Friends Everywhere

Table of Contents

INTRODUCTION

*I*n your hands, you hold a book entitled *Promises and Prayers for Friends*. Perhaps you received this book as a gift from a trusted friend, or perhaps you picked it up on your own. Either way, you will be blessed *if* you take the words of these pages to heart.

This text addresses 72 topics. Each brief chapter contains Bible verses, a quotation from a noted Christian thinker, and a prayer. The ideas in each chapter are powerful reminders of God's commandments and the joys of Christian friendship.

Genuine, lifelong friendship is ordained by God. As such, it should be valued and nurtured. As Christians, we are commanded to love one another, and the familiar words of 1st Corinthians 13:13 remind us that love and charity are among God's greatest gifts: *But now faith, hope, love, abide these three; but the greatest of these is love.* (NASB)

Today and every day, resolve to be a trustworthy, encouraging, loyal friend. And, while you're at it, treasure the people in your life who are loyal friends to you. Friendship is, after all, a glorious gift, praised by God. Give thanks for that gift and make it grow.

>⊹—◆—○—◆—⊹<

ABUNDANCE

...these things I speak in the world, that they might have my joy fulfilled in themselves.

—John 17:13 KJV

...I am come that they might have life, and that they might have it more abundantly.

—John 10:10 KJV

Commit to the Lord whatever you do, and your plans will succeed.

—Proverbs 16:3 NIV

But as for you, be strong and do not give up, for your work will be rewarded.

—II Chronicles 15:7 NIV

His lord said unto him, Well done, thou good and faithful servant: thou hast been faithful over a few things, I will make thee ruler over many things: enter thou into the joy of thy lord.

—Matthew 25:21 KJV

*T*he familiar words of *John 10:10* remind us that Jesus offers the abundant life to all who believe in Him. Today, let us accept God's promise of spiritual abundance. And then, in a spirit of optimism and faith, let us share our abundance with all who cross our paths.

><+><>+<+><

We honor God by asking for great things when they are a part of His promise. We dishonor Him and cheat ourselves when we ask for molehills where He has promised mountains.

—Vance Havner

—A PRAYER—

*H*eavenly Father, You have promised an abundant life through Your Son Jesus. Thank You, Lord, for Your abundance. Guide me according to Your will, so that I might be a worthy servant in all that I say and do, this day and every day.

—Amen

ACCEPTING CHRIST

For God so loved the world, that he gave his only begotten Son, that whosoever believeth in him should not perish, but have everlasting life.

—John 3:16 KJV

For the wages of sin is death, but the gift of God is eternal life in Christ Jesus our Lord.

—Romans 6:23 NIV

He saved us, not on the basis of deeds which we have done in righteousness, but according to His mercy, by the washing of regeneration and renewing by the Holy Spirit, whom He poured out upon us richly through Jesus Christ our Savior....

—Titus 3:5-6 NASB

Jesus answered and said unto her, Whosoever drinketh of this water shall thirst again: but whosoever drinketh of the water that I shall give him shall never thirst; but the water that I shall give him shall be in him a well of water springing up into everlasting life.

—John 4:13-14 KJV

God's love for you is so great that He sent His only Son to this earth to die for your sins and offer you the priceless gift of eternal life. You must decide whether or not to accept God's gift. The decision, of course, is yours and yours alone, and it has eternal consequences. Accept God's gift: Accept Christ.

>─◆─○─◆─<

What do you think God wants you to do? The answer is that He wants you to turn to Jesus and open your life to Him.

—Billy Graham

—A Prayer—

Heavenly Father, when you invited me to be part of Your family, I said yes. I accepted Jesus as my Lord and Savior, and You saved me. Today, let me live in such a way that others might also know Christ as their Savior and that they might see my love for You reflected in my words and my deeds.

—Amen

ADVERSITY

He heals the brokenhearted, and binds their wounds.

—Psalm 147:3 NASB

I tell you the truth, you will weep and mourn while the world rejoices. You will grieve, but your grief will turn to joy.

—John 16:20 NIV

He restoreth my soul: he leadeth me in the paths of righteousness for his name's sake.

—Psalm 23:3 KJV

…be of good cheer; I have overcome the world.

—John 16:33 KJV

A time to weep, and a time to laugh; a time to mourn, and a time to dance….

—Ecclesiastes 3:4 KJV

*F*rom time to time, all of us face adversity. During the most difficult days of our lives, God stands ready to protect us. As *Psalm 147* promises, "He heals the brokenhearted...." And, in His own time and according to His master plan, He will heal you if you invite Him into your heart.

⋗─┼─◈─○─◈─┼─⋖

The kingdom of God is a kingdom of paradox, where through the ugly defeat of a cross, a holy God is utterly glorified. Victory comes through defeat; healing through brokenness; finding self through losing self.

—Chuck Colsen

—A Prayer—

*D*ear Lord, when I am troubled, You heal me. When I am afraid, You protect me. When I am discouraged, You lift me up. You are my unending source of strength, Lord; let me turn to You when I am weak, and give me faith in the promise of Your healing power.

—Amen

ANGER

A patient man has great understanding, but a quick-tempered man displays folly.

—Proverbs 14:29 NIV

But I tell you that anyone who is angry with his brother is subject to judgement.

—Matthew 5:22 NIV

Make no friendship with an angry man....

—Proverbs 22:24 KJV

Refrain from anger and turn from wrath; do not fret—it leads only to evil.

—Psalm 37:8 NIV

....do not let the sun go down on your anger, and do not give the devil an opportunity.

—Ephesians 4:26-27 NASB

*A*nger is a natural human emotion that is sometimes necessary and appropriate. Even Jesus Himself became angered when He confronted the money changers in the temple. But, more often than not, our frustrations are of the more mundane variety. When you are tempted to lose your temper over the minor inconveniences of life, don't. Turn away from anger, and turn instead to God.

><+>+O+<+><

Peace is the deepest thing a human personality can know, it is almighty.

—*Oswald Chambers*

—A PRAYER—

*D*ear Lord, I am an imperfect human being, sometimes quick to anger and sometimes slow to forgive. When I fall prey to pettiness, restore my sense of perspective. When I fall prey to anger, give me inner calm. When I am slow to forgive, Lord, keep me mindful of Your commandment that I should love my neighbor as myself. And, as I turn away from anger, let me claim for myself the peace that You intend for my life.

—*Amen*

ATTITUDE

You were taught, with regard to your former way of life, to put off your old self, which is being corrupted by its deceitful desires; to be made new in the attitude of your minds; and to put on the new self, created to be like God in true righteousness and holiness.

—*Ephesians 4:22-24 NIV*

Set your mind on the things above, not on the things that are on earth.

—*Colossians 3:2 NASB*

Your attitude should be the same as that of Christ Jesus: Who, being in very nature God, did not consider equality with God something to be grasped, but made himself nothing, taking the very nature of a servant, being made in human likeness. And being found in appearance as a man, he humbled himself and became obedient to death—even death on a cross!

—*Philippians 2:5-8 NIV*

As Christians, we have every reason to rejoice. God is in His heaven; Christ has risen, and we are the sheep of His flock. Today, let us count our blessings instead of our hardships. And, let us thank the Giver of all things good for gifts that are simply too numerous to count.

⊰━◆◈━◦━◈◆━⊱

Attitude is all-important. Let the soul take a quiet attitude of faith and love toward God, and from there on the responsibility is God's. He will make good on His commitments.

—*A. W. Tozer*

—A Prayer—

Lord...I pray for an attitude that is Christlike. Whatever the circumstances I face, whether good or bad, triumphal or tragic, may my response reflect a God-honoring, Christlike attitude of optimism, faith, and love for You.

—*Amen*

BEHAVIOR

Teach me your ways, O Lord, that I may live according to your truth! Grant me purity of heart, that I may honor you.

—Psalm 86:11 NLT

For the Lord God is our light and our protector. He gives us grace and glory. No good thing will the Lord withhold from those who do what is right. O Lord Almighty, happy are those who trust in you.

—Psalm 84:11-12 NLT

Let us walk honestly, as in the day; not in rioting and drunkenness, not in chambering and wantonness, not in strife and envying.

—Romans 13:13 KJV

Jesus answered and said unto him, If a man love me, he will keep my words: and my Father will love him, and we will come unto him, and make our abode with him.

—John 14:23 KJV

*D*ecisions, decisions, decisions…We have so many decisions each day and so many opportunities to stray from God's commandments. When we live according to God's commandments and follow His will, we earn for ourselves the abundance and peace that God intends for our lives.

>—◆>—O—<◆>—<

There may be no trumpet sound or loud applause when we make a right decision, just a calm sense of resolution and peace.

—*Gloria Gaither*

—A PRAYER—

*L*ord, I pray that my actions will always be consistent with my beliefs. I know that my deeds speak more loudly than my words. May every step that I take reflect Your truth and love, and may others be drawn to You because of my words and my deeds.

—*Amen*

THE BIBLE

Heaven and earth will pass away, but my words will never pass away.

—*Matthew 24:35 NIV*

Whosoever cometh to me, and heareth my sayings, and doeth them, I will show you to whom he is like: he is like a man which built a house, and digged deep, and laid the foundation on a rock: and when the flood arose, the stream beat vehemently upon that house, and could not shake it; for it was founded upon a rock.

—*Luke 6:47-48 KJV*

But he answered and said, It is written, Man shall not live by bread alone but by every word that proceedeth out of the mouth of God.

—*Matthew 4:4 KJV*

Every word of God is flawless; he is a shield to those who take refuge in him.

—*Proverbs 30:5 NIV*

*G*od has given us the Holy Bible so that we might know His commandments, His wisdom, His love, and His Son. When we study God's teachings and apply them to our lives, we live by the Word that shall never pass away.

⊱━⊰◦⊱━⊰

If you see a Bible that is falling apart, it probably belongs to someone who isn't.

—*Vance Havner*

—A PRAYER—

*D*ear Lord, the Bible is Your gift to me; let me use it. When I stray from Your Holy Word, Lord, I suffer. But, when I place Your Word at the very center of my life, I am blessed. Make me a faithful student of Your Word.

—*Amen*

CHARACTER

The man of integrity walks securely, but he who takes crooked paths will be found out.

—Proverbs 10:9 NIV

In everything set them an example by doing what is good. In your teaching show integrity, seriousness and soundness of speech that cannot be condemned, so that those who oppose you may be ashamed because they have nothing bad to say about us.

—Titus 2:7 NIV

…Abhor that which is evil; cleave to that which is good.

—Romans 12: 9 KJV

Blessed is the man that walketh not in the counsel of the ungodly, nor standeth in the way of sinners, nor sitteth in the seat of the scornful.

—Psalm 1:1 KJV

Character is built slowly over a lifetime. It is the sum of every right decision, every honest word, every noble thought, and every heartfelt prayer. It is forged on the anvil of honorable work and polished by the twin virtues of generosity and humility. Character is a precious thing—difficult to build but easy to tear down. Protect it always.

⋙—◦—⋘

There is no way to grow a saint overnight. Character, like the oak tree, does not spring up like a mushroom.

—Vance Havner

—A Prayer—

Lord…You are my Father in Heaven. You search my heart and know me far better than I know myself. May I be Your worthy servant, and may I live according to Your commandments. Let me be a person of integrity, Lord, and let my words and deeds be a testimony to You, today and always.

—Amen

CHEERFULNESS

I will thank you, Lord with all my heart; I will tell of all the marvelous things you have done. I will be filled with joy because of you. I will sing praises to your name, O Most High.

—*Psalm 9:1-2 NLT*

Make me to hear joy and gladness....

—*Psalm 51:8 KJV*

I will praise the name of God with a song, and will magnify him with thanksgiving.

—*Psalm 69:30 KJV*

Set your mind on the things above, not on the things that are on earth.

—*Colossians 3:2 NASB*

These things have I spoken unto you, that my joy might remain in you, and that your joy might be full.

—*John 15:11 KJV*

Few things in life are more sad, or, for that matter, more absurd, than a grumpy Christian. Christ promises us a life of abundance and joy, but He does not force His joy upon us. We must claim His joy for ourselves.

><+>-0-<+><

Joy is the serious business of heaven.

—*C. S. Lewis*

—A Prayer—

Dear Lord, You have given me so many reasons to celebrate. Today, let me choose an attitude of cheerfulness. Let me be a joyful Christian, Lord, quick to smile and slow to anger. And, let me share Your goodness with all whom I meet so that Your love might shine in me and through me.

—*Amen*

CONSCIENCE

And do not be conformed to this world, but be transformed by the renewing of your mind, that you may prove what is that good and acceptable and perfect will of God.

—Romans 12:2 NKJV

This being so, I myself always strive to have a conscience without offense toward God and men.

—Acts 24:16 NKJV

Since, then, you have been raised with Christ, set your hearts on things above, where Christ is seated at the right hand of God. Set your minds on things above, not on earthly things.

—Colossians 3:1,2 NIV

…let us draw near to God with a sincere heart in full assurance of faith, having our hearts sprinkled to cleanse us from a guilty conscience and having our bodies washed with pure water.

—Hebrews 10:22 NIV

A clear conscience is the reward we earn when we obey God's Word and follow His will. When we follow God's commandments, our earthly rewards are never-ceasing, and our heavenly rewards are everlasting.

><*><•><O><•><*><

My conscience is captive to the word of God.
—*Martin Luther*

—A PRAYER—

*D*ear Lord…You speak to me through the Bible, through teachers, and through friends. And, Father, through that still small voice, You reveal Your will and Your way for my life. In these quiet moments, show me Your plan for this day, that I might serve You.

—*Amen*

CONTENTMENT

I know what it is to be in need, and I know what it is to have plenty. I have learned the secret of being content in any and every situation, whether well fed or hungry, whether living in plenty or in want. I can do everything through him who gives me strength.

—Philippians 4:12,13 NIV

And all things are of God, who hath reconciled us to himself by Jesus Christ, and hath given to us the ministry of reconciliation....

—II Corinthians 5:18 KJV

A happy heart makes the face cheerful, but heartache crushes the spirit.

—Proverbs 15:13 NIV

Peace I leave with you, my peace I give unto you; not as the world giveth, give I unto you. Let not your heart be troubled, neither let it be afraid.

—John 14 27 KJV

Be still, and know that I am God....

—Psalm 46:10 KJV

Where can we find contentment? Is it a result of wealth, or power, or fame? Hardly. Genuine contentment is a gift from God to those who trust in Him and follow His commandments. When God dwells at the center of our lives, contentment will belong to us just as surely as we belong to God.

><+>-O-<+><

If we know we have pleased God, contentment will be our consolation, for what pleases God will please us.

—*Kay Arthur*

—A Prayer—

Father…You are my contentment. Whatever my circumstances, I find contentment whenever I seek Your healing hand. Let me look to You, today, Father, for the peace that You have offered me through the gift of Your Son.

—*Amen*

COURAGE

The Lord is my light and my salvation; whom shall I fear? The Lord is the strength of my life; of whom shall I be afraid?

—*Psalm 27:1 KJV*

Be of good courage, and he shall strengthen your heart, all ye that hope in the Lord.

—*Psalm 31:24 KJV*

But Jesus beheld them, and said unto them, "With men this is impossible; but with God all things are possible."

—*Matthew 19:26 KJV*

I can do everything through him that gives me strength.

—*Philippians 4:13 NIV*

In thee, O Lord, do I put my trust; let me never be put into confusion.

—*Psalm 71:1 KJV*

From time to time, all of us, even the most devout believers, experience fear. But, as Christians, we are protected by a loving God and a living Savior. The ultimate battle has already been won at Calvary. We, as believers, can live courageously in the promises of our Lord…and we should.

><+>•O•<+><

The truth of Christ brings assurance and so removes the former problem of fear and uncertainty.

—*A. W. Tozer*

—A Prayer—

Dear Lord, sometimes I face disappointments and challenges that leave me worried and afraid. When I am fearful, let me seek Your strength. When I am anxious, give me faith. Keep me mindful, Lord, that with You by my side, I have nothing to fear. Help me to be Your grateful and courageous servant this day and every day.

—*Amen*

COURTESY

Use hospitality one to another without grudging.

—*I Peter 4:9 KJV*

A soft answer turneth away wrath: but grievous words stir up anger.

—*Proverbs 15:1 KJV*

A kind man benefits himself, but a cruel man brings trouble on himself.

—*Proverbs 11:17 NIV*

Be gentle unto all men, apt to teach, patient.

—*II Timothy 2:24 KJV*

And be ye kind one to another, tenderhearted, forgiving one another, even as God for Christ's sake hath forgiven you.

—*Ephesians 4:32 KJV*

*D*id Christ instruct us in matters of etiquette and courtesy? Of course He did. Christ's instructions are crystal clear: *In everything, therefore, treat people the same way you want them to treat you, for this is the Law and the Prophets.* (Matthew 7:12 NASB) May we all use The Golden Rule as our guide for the treatment of others.

~>―◆>―0―<◆―<~

What is your focus today? Joy comes when it is Jesus first, others second...then you.

—*Kay Arthur*

—A Prayer—

*G*uide me this day, O Lord, to treat everyone I meet with courtesy and respect. You have created each person in Your own image; let me honor those who cross my path with the dignity that You have bestowed upon them. We are all Your children, Lord; let me show kindness to Your children.

—*Amen*

Encouraging Others

But encourage one another day after day, as long as it is still called "Today," so that none of you will be hardened by the deceitfulness of sin.

—Hebrews 3:13 NASB

Let the word of Christ dwell in you richly in all wisdom; teaching and admonishing one another in psalms and hymns and spiritual songs, singing with grace in your hearts to the Lord.

—Colossians 3:16 KJV

Be kindly affectioned one to another with brotherly love; in honor preferring one another; not slothful in business; fervent in spirit; serving the Lord; rejoicing in hope; patient in tribulation; continuing instant in prayer....

—Romans 12:10-12 KJV

...I tell you the truth, whatever you did for one of the least of these brothers of mine, you did for me.

—Matthew 25:40 NIV

$\mathcal{L}$ife is a team sport, and we all need encouraging teammates. Encouragement is paradoxical: the more we give to others, the more we keep for ourselves. When we spread the gift of encouragement to our family and friends, they win…and so do we.

⇒⇥◆⇥◦⇤◆⇤⇐

Encouragement is the oxygen of the soul.

—*John Maxwell*

—A PRAYER—

$\mathcal{D}$ear Lord, You have loved me, cared for me, encouraged me, and saved me. Make me ever-grateful for Your grace. And just as You have lifted me up, let me also lift up others in a spirit of encouragement and hope. Today, let me share the healing message of Your Son, and in doing so, care for brothers and sisters in need. And, to whatever extent I can be of service to others, Lord, may the glory be Yours.

—*Amen*

ETERNAL LIFE

Jesus answered and said to her, "Everyone who drinks of this water will thirst again; but whoever drinks of the water that I will give him shall never thirst; but the water that I will give him will become in him a well of water springing up to eternal life."

—John 4:13-14 NASB

For God so loved the world, that he gave his only begotten Son, that whosoever believeth in him should not perish, but have everlasting life.

—John 3:16 KJV

For if ye live after the flesh, ye shall die: but if ye through the Spirit do mortify the deeds of the body, ye shall live.

—Romans 8:13 KJV

Surely goodness and mercy shall follow me all the days of my life: and I will dwell in the house of the LORD for ever.

—Psalm 23:6 KJV

*C*hrist died on the cross so that we might have eternal life. This gift, freely given from God's only begotten Son, is the priceless possession of everyone who accepts Him as Lord and Savior. Claim Christ's gift today.

>—+—◆—+—○—+—◆—+—<

God loves you and wants you to experience peace and life—abundant and eternal.

—*Billy Graham*

—A Prayer—

I know, Lord, this world is not my home; I am only here for a brief while. You have given me the priceless gift of eternal life through Your Son Jesus. Keep the hope of heaven fresh in my heart. While I am in this world, help me to pass through it with faith in my heart and praise on my lips for You.

—*Amen*

EVIL

Submit yourselves therefore to God. Resist the devil, and he will flee from you. Draw nigh to God, and he will draw nigh to you.

—*James 4:7-8 KJV*

The wicked say to themselves, "God isn't watching! He will never notice!"

—*Psalm 10:11 NLT*

A fool finds pleasure in evil conduct, but a man of understanding delights in wisdom.

—*Proverbs 10:23 NIV*

Create in me a clean heart, O God; and renew a right spirit within me.

—*Psalm 51:10 KJV*

But now being made free from sin, and become servants to God, ye have your fruit unto holiness, and the end everlasting life. For the wages of sin is death; but the gift of God is eternal life through Jesus Christ our Lord.

—*Romans 6:22-23 KJV*

This world is God's creation, and it contains the wonderful fruits of His handiwork. But, it also contains countless opportunities to stray from God's will. Temptations are everywhere, and the devil, it seems, never takes a day off. Our task, as believers, is to turn away from temptation and to place our lives squarely in the center of God's will. When we do, evil can never conquer us.

Of two evils, choose neither.

—*C. H. Spurgeon*

—A Prayer—

Strengthen my walk with You, my heavenly Father. Evil comes in so many disguises that sometimes it is only with Your help that I can recognize right from wrong. Your presence in my life enables me to choose truth and to live a life pleasing to You. May I always live in Your presence.

—*Amen*

FAITH

…for truly I say to you, if you have faith as a mustard seed, you shall say to this mountain, "Move from here to there," and it shall move; and nothing shall be impossible to you.

—*Matthew 17:20 NASB*

Trust in him at all times, O people; pour out your hearts to him, for God is our refuge.

—*Psalm 62:8 NIV*

The Lord's lovingkindnesses indeed never cease, for His compassions never fail. They are new every morning. Great is Thy faithfulness.

—*Lamentations 3:22-23 NASB*

For in the gospel a righteousness is being revealed, a righteousness that is by faith from first to last, just as it is written: "The righteous will live by faith."

—*Romans 1:17 NIV*

*H*ave you, on occasion, felt your faith in God slipping away? If so, welcome to the club. We, as mere mortals, are subject to emotions like fear, worry, and doubt. When we fall short of perfect faith, God understands us and forgives us. And, God stands ready to strengthen us, to bless us, and to renew us *if* we turn our doubts and fears over to Him.

>─◆─○─◆─<

If I should neglect prayer but a single day, I should lose a great deal of the fire of faith.

—*Martin Luther*

—A Prayer—

*D*ear God, sometimes this world can be a fearful place, full of uncertainty and doubt. In those dark moments, help me to remember that You are always near and that You can overcome any challenge. Give me faith and let me remember always that with Your love and Your power, I can live courageously and faithfully today and every day.

—*Amen*

FORGIVENESS

Be ye therefore merciful, as your Father also is merciful.

—Luke 6:36 KJV

He who covers over an offense promotes love, but whoever repeats the matter separates close friends.

—Proverbs 17:9 NIV

Then came Peter to him, and said, Lord, how oft shall my brother sin against me, and I forgive him? till seven times? Jesus saith unto him, I say not unto thee, Until seven times: but, Until seventy times seven.

—Matthew 18:21-22 KJV

So in everything, do to others what you would have them do to you, for this sums up the Law and the Prophets.

—Matthew 7:12 NIV

Blessed are the merciful: for they shall obtain mercy.

—Matthew 5:7 KJV

Forgiveness is God's commandment, but being frail, fallible, imperfect human beings, we are quick to anger, quick to blame, slow to forgive, and even slower to forget. No matter. Forgiveness is God's way, and it must be our way, too. If there exists even one person, alive or dead, whom you have not forgiven (and that includes yourself), follow God's commandment and His will for your life: forgive. Hatred and bitterness and regret are not part of God's plan for your life. Forgiveness is.

>─┤◆├─○─┤◆├─<

God forgets the past. Imitate him.

—*Max Lucado*

—A Prayer—

Heavenly Father, I know forgiveness is Your commandment, but genuine forgiveness is difficult indeed. Help me to forgive others, Lord, just as You have forgiven me. And keep me mindful, Dear God, that I am never fully liberated until I have been freed from the shackles of hatred. Let me be a forgiving Christian, Dear Lord, today and always.

—*Amen*

FRIENDSHIP

A friend loves at all times....

—Proverbs 17:17 NIV

Thine own friend, and thy father's friend, forsake not....

—Proverbs 27:10 KJV

Happy are those who deal justly with others and always do what is right.

—Psalm 106:3 NLT

In everything, therefore, treat people the same way you want them to treat you, for this is the Law and the Prophets.

—Matthew 7:12 NASB

As we have therefore opportunity, let us do good unto all men....

—Galatians 6:10 KJV

*T*oday, resolve to be a trustworthy, encouraging, loyal friend. And, treasure the people in your life who are loyal friends to you. Friendship is, after all, a glorious gift, praised by God. Give thanks for that gift and nurture it.

❦

Friendship is one of the sweetest joys of life. Many might have failed beneath the bitterness of their trial had they not found a friend.

—*C. H. Spurgeon*

—A Prayer—

*L*ord, You seek abundance and joy for me and for all Your children. One way that I can share Your joy is through the gift of friendship. Help me to be a loyal friend, Lord. Let me be ready to listen, ready to encourage, and ready to offer a helping hand. Keep me mindful that I am a servant of Your Son Christ Jesus, and may the love of Jesus shine through me today and forever.

—*Amen*

GENEROSITY

Do not withhold good from those who deserve it when it is within your power to act.

—Proverbs 3:27 NIV

Freely you have received, freely give.

—Matthew 10:8 NIV

He that hath two coats, let him impart to him that hath none; and he that hath meat, let him do likewise.

—Luke 3:11 KJV

And let us not be weary in well doing: for in due season we shall reap, if we faint not.

—Galatians 6:9 KJV

And above all things have fervent charity among yourselves: for charity shall cover the multitude of sins.

—I Peter 4:8 KJV

As believers in Christ, our blessings are simply too numerous to count. But, even if we can't *enumerate* our blessings, we can *reciprocate* by showing kindness and generosity to those who cross our paths.

⇒—◆⟫—O—⟪◆—⇐

We are never more like God than when we give.
—*Chuck Swindoll*

—A Prayer—

Lord, You have been so generous with me; let me be generous with others. Help me to be generous with my time and my possessions as I care for those in need. And, make me a humble giver, Lord, so that all the glory and the praise might be Yours.

—*Amen*

GIFTS

Now there are varieties of gifts, but the same Spirit. And there are varieties of ministries, and the same Lord.

—*1 Corinthians 12: 4-5 NASB*

Every good gift and every perfect gift is from above, and cometh down from the Father of lights.

—*James 1:17 KJV*

Since we have gifts that differ according to the grace given to us, *each of us is to exercise them accordingly:* if prophecy, according to the proportion of his faith; if service, in his serving; or he who teaches, in his teaching; or he who exhorts, in his exhortation; he who gives, with liberality; he who leads, with diligence; he who shows mercy, with cheerfulness.

—*Romans 12:6-8 NASB*

Neglect not the gift that is in thee....

—*I Timothy 4:14 KJV*

*Y*our talents are a gift from God: Use them. And encourage your family and friends to do likewise. God intends that we all use our talents for the glory of His kingdom. The best way to say "Thank You" for God's gifts is to use them.

><+>·O·<+><

You are the only person on earth who can use your ability.

—Zig Ziglar

—A Prayer—

*L*ord, You have blessed me with a love that is far beyond my limited understanding. You loved me before I was ever born; You sent Your Son Jesus to redeem me from my sins; You have given me the gift of eternal life. And, You have given me special talents; let me use those talents to the best of my ability and to the glory of Your kingdom so that I might be a good and faithful servant this day and forever.

—Amen

God's Grace

...for all have sinned and fall short of the glory of God, and are justified freely by his grace through the redemption that came by Christ Jesus.

—*Romans 3:23,24 NIV*

In Him we have redemption through His blood, the forgiveness of sins, according to the riches of His grace which He made to abound toward us in all wisdom and prudence....

—*Ephesians 1:7,8 KJV*

As God's fellow workers we urge you not to receive God's grace in vain. For he says, "In the time of my favor I heard you, and in the day of salvation I helped you. I tell you, now is the time of God's favor, now is the day of salvation."

—*2 Corinthians 6:1,2 NIV*

For it is by grace you have been saved, through faith—and this not from yourselves, it is the gift of God—not by works, so that no one can boast.

—*Ephesians 2:8,9 NIV*

We have not earned our salvation; it is a gift from God. When we accept Christ as our Savior, we are saved by God's grace. Let us praise God for His gift, and let us share the Good News with all who cross our paths.

✦

We are here to be living monuments of God's grace.

—*Oswald Chambers*

—A PRAYER—

Accepting Your grace can be hard, Lord. Somehow, I feel that I must earn Your love and Your acceptance. Yet, the Bible makes this glorious promise: You love me and save me by Your grace. It is a gift I can only accept and not earn. Thank You for Your gift of grace.

—*Amen*

GOD'S LOVE

But the love of the Lord remains forever with those who fear him. His salvation extends to the children's children of those who are faithful to his covenant, of those who obey his commandments!

—*Psalm 103:17-18 NLT*

For God so loved the world, that he gave his only begotten Son, that whosoever believeth in him should not perish, but have everlasting life.

—*John 3:16 KJV*

For I am persuaded, that neither death, nor life, nor angels, nor principalities, nor powers, nor things present, nor things to come, nor height, nor depth, nor any other creature, shall be able to separate us from the love of God, which is in Christ Jesus our Lord.

—*Romans 8:38-39 KJV*

For the Lord is good. His unfailing love continues forever, and his faithfulness continues to each generation.

—*Psalm 100:5 NLT*

God is a loving Father. We, as God's faithful children, are called upon to return His love *and* to follow His commandments. When we do, we are blessed…and the Father smiles.

><+>-o-<+><

God loves each of us as if there were only one of us.

—*St. Augustine*

—A Prayer—

Thank You, Lord, for Your love. Your love is boundless, infinite, and eternal. Today, let me pause and reflect upon Your love for me, and let me share that love with all those who cross my path. And, as an expression of my love for You, Lord, let me share the saving message of Your Son Jesus with a world in desperate need of His peace.

—*Amen*

God's Mercy

For the LORD your God is a merciful God....

—*Deuteronomy 4:31 NIV*

The LORD is gracious and full of compassion, Slow to anger and great in mercy. The LORD is good to all, And His tender mercies are over all His works.

—*Psalm 145:8,9 NKJV*

Be merciful, just as your Father is merciful.

—*Luke 6:36 NIV*

Blessed be the God and Father of our Lord Jesus Christ, who according to His abundant mercy has begotten us again to a living hope through the resurrection of Jesus Christ from the dead....

—*1 Peter 1:3 NKJV*

He has showed you, O man, what is good. And what does the LORD require of you? To act justly and to love mercy and to walk humbly with your God.

—*Micah 6:8 NIV*

God is merciful, and His love is beyond human understanding; He sent His only Son to die for our sins so that we might have the gift of eternal life. We must praise God always and thank Him for His gifts. One way that we thank God is to share His love and His mercy with all who cross our paths.

⊱•◦—○—◦•⊰

The great love of God is an ocean without a bottom or a shore.

—C. H. Spurgeon

—A Prayer—

Dear Lord, You have graced me with so much more than I deserve. You have blessed me with Your love and Your mercy. Enable me to be merciful toward others, Father, just as You have been merciful to me, and let me share Your love with all whom I meet.

—Amen

GOD'S PLAN

Trust the Lord your God with all your heart and lean not on your own understanding; in all your ways acknowledge him, and he will make your paths straight.

—Proverbs 3:5-6 NIV

For every house is built by someone, but the builder of all things is God.

—Hebrews 3:4 NASB

The Lord says, "I will guide you along the best pathway for your life. I will advise you and watch over you."

—Psalm 32:8 NLT

The steps of a good man are ordered by the LORD....

—Psalm 37:23 KJV

The Lord is good and does what is right; he shows the proper path to those who go astray.

—Psalm 25:8 NLT

*G*od has plans for you…big plans. To understand those plans, you must study God's Word and seek His will for your life. When you do, you'll be amazed at the marvelous things that God will do.

❦

We should not be upset when unexpected and upsetting things happen. God, in his wisdom, means to make something of us which we have not yet attained, and He is dealing with us accordingly.

—J. I. Packer

—A Prayer—

*L*ord, You have a plan for my life that is grander than I can imagine. Let Your purposes be my purposes. Let Your will be my will. When I am confused, give me clarity. When I am frightened, give me courage. Let me be Your faithful servant, always seeking Your guidance for my life. And let me always be a shining beacon for Your Son, Christ Jesus today and every day that I live.

—Amen

GOD'S SUPPORT

The Lord is my shepherd; I shall not want.

—*Psalm 23:1 KJV*

Every word of God is flawless; he is a shield to those who take refuge in him.

—*Proverbs 30:5 NIV*

Give us help from trouble: for vain is the help of man.

—*Psalm 60:11 KJV*

He giveth power to the faint; and to them that have no might he increaseth strength.

—*Isaiah 40:29 KJV*

For the eyes of the Lord are toward the righteous, and his ears attend to their prayers.

—*1 Peter 3: 12 NASB*

God loves us and protects us. In times of trouble, He comforts us; in times of sorrow, He dries our tears. When we are troubled, or weak, or sorrowful, God is as near as our next breath. Let us build our lives on the rock that cannot be shaken...let us trust in God.

>—⬧—○—⬥—<

God walks with us....He scoops us up in His arms or simply sits with us in silent strength until we cannot avoid the awesome recognition that yes, even now, He is here.

—*Gloria Gaither*

—A PRAYER—

Lord...You have promised never to leave me or forsake me. You are always with me, protecting me and encouraging me. Whatever this day may bring, I thank You for Your love and Your strength. Let me lean upon You, Father, this day and forever.

—*Amen*

GOD'S TIMING

He has made everything beautiful in its time. He has also set eternity in the hearts of men; yet they cannot fathom what God has done from beginning to end.

—Ecclesiastes 3:11 NIV

Wait for the LORD; be strong and take heart and wait for the LORD.

—Psalm 27:14 NIV

He said to them: "It is not for you to know the times or dates the Father has set by his own authority."

—Acts 1:7 NIV

The steps of the Godly are directed by the Lord. He delights in every detail of their lives. Though they stumble, they will not fall, for the Lord holds them by the hand.

—Psalm 37:23-24 NLT

I waited patiently for the LORD; And He inclined to me, And heard my cry.

—Psalm 40:1 NKJV

We human beings are impatient. We know what we want, and we know exactly when we want it: NOW! But, God knows better. He has created a world that unfolds according to His own timetable, not ours. Let us be patient as we wait for God to reveal the glorious plans that He has for our lives.

⤖⊶⊙⊷⤛

God never hurries. There are no deadlines against which He must work. To know this is to quiet our spirits and relax our nerves.

—*A. W. Tozer*

—A Prayer—

Lord...Your timing is seldom my timing, but Your timing is always right for me. You are my Father, and You have a plan for my life that is grander than I can imagine. When I am impatient, remind me that You are never early or late. You are always on time, Lord, so let me trust in You...always.

—*Amen*

GOLDEN RULE

Therefore all things whatsoever ye would that men should do to you, do ye even so to them: for this is the law and the prophets.

—Matthew 7:12 KJV

As we have therefore opportunity, let us do good unto all men, especially unto them who are of the household of faith.

—Galatians 6:10 KJV

Be kindly affectioned one to another with brotherly love; in honor preferring one another; not slothful in business; fervent in spirit; serving the Lord; rejoicing in hope; patient in tribulation; continuing instant in prayer....

—Romans 12:10-12 KJV

...I tell you the truth, whatever you did for one of the least of these brothers of mine, you did for me.

—Matthew 25:40 NIV

*T*he familiar words found in *Matthew 7:12* remind us that, as followers of Christ, we are commanded to treat others as we wish to be treated. This commandment is, indeed, the Golden Rule for Christians of every generation. When we weave the thread of kindness into the very fabric of our lives, we give glory to the One who gave His life for us.

>——◦——<

If my heart is right with God, every human being is my neighbor.

—*Oswald Chambers*

—A Prayer—

*F*ather...help me always to do for my friends as I would want my friends to do for me. Let me rejoice in their strengths, and let me overlook their weaknesses, just as they overlook mine. And, in all my dealings, may I be guided by the love of Christ that I feel in my heart.

—*Amen*

GRATITUDE

Therefore, since we receive a kingdom which cannot be shaken, let us show gratitude by which we may offer to God an acceptable service with reverence and awe....

—Hebrews 12:28 NASB

Bless the LORD, O my soul, and forget not all his benefits....

—Psalm 103:2 KJV

In everything give thanks; for this is God's will for you in Christ Jesus.

—I Thessalonians 5:18 NIV

This is the day which the Lord hath made; we will rejoice and be glad in it.

—Psalm 118:24 KJV

And let the peace of God rule in your hearts...and be ye thankful.

—Colossians 3:15 KJV

As children, we are taught to say "please" and "thank you." And, as adults, we should approach God in the same way. We should offer up our needs to Him in prayer ("Please, Dear Lord...."), and we should graciously give thanks for the gifts He has given us. Let us praise God and thank Him. He is the Giver of all things good.

⊱⸺◦⸺⊰

It is only with gratitude that life becomes rich.
—Dietrich Bonhoeffer

—A Prayer—

Dear Lord, I want my attitude to be one of gratitude. You have given me much, even when I deserve so little. When I think of Your grace and goodness to me, I am humbled and thankful. Today, let me express my gratitude, Lord, not just through my words but also through my deeds. And may all the glory be Yours.

—Amen

GRIEF

Blessed are those who mourn, for they will be comforted.

—*Matthew 5:4 NIV*

They that sow in tears shall reap in joy.

—*Psalm 126:5 KJV*

I cried out to the Lord in my suffering, and he heard me. He set me free from all my fears.

—*Psalm 34:6 NLT*

…weeping may remain for a night, but rejoicing comes in the morning.

—*Psalm 30:5 NIV*

These things I have spoken unto you, that in me ye might have peace. In the world ye shall have tribulation: but be of good cheer; I have overcome the world.

—*John 16:33 KJV*

All of us experience adversity and pain. When we lose something—or someone—we love, we grieve our losses. During times of heartache—or heartbreak—we can turn to God for solace. When we do, He comforts us and, in time, He heals us.

<hr />

The grace of God is sufficient for all our needs, for every problem and for every difficulty, for every broken heart, and for every human sorrow.

—Peter Marshall

—A Prayer—

You have promised, Lord, that You will not give me any more than I can bear. You have promised to lift me up out of my grief and despair. You have promised to put a new song on my lips. I thank You, Lord, for sustaining me in my day of sorrow. Restore me, and heal me, and use me as You will.

—Amen

HAPPINESS

Happy are those who fear the Lord. Yes, happy are those who delight in doing his commands.

—*Psalm 112:1 NLT*

Happy is he...whose hope is in the Lord his God.

—*Psalm 146:5 KJV*

Happy is the man that findeth wisdom, and the man that getteth understanding.

—*Proverbs 3:13 KJV*

Delight thyself also in the LORD; and he shall give thee the desires of thine heart.

—*Psalm 37:4 KJV*

...I am come that they might have life, and that they might have it more abundantly.

—*John 10:10 KJV*

*H*appiness depends less upon our circumstances than upon our thoughts. When we turn our thoughts to God, to His gifts, and to His glorious creation, we experience the joy that God intends for His children. But, when we focus on the negative aspects of life, we suffer needlessly. Today and every day, let us turn our thoughts—and our hearts—to God.

⊳—◇—⊴

The happiest people in the world are not those who have no problems, but the people who have learned to live with those things that are less than perfect.

—James Dobson

—A Prayer—

*D*ear Lord…You are my strength and my joy. I will rejoice in the day that You have made, and I will give thanks for the countless blessings that You have given me. Let me be a joyful Christian, Lord, as I share the Good News of Your Son. And let me praise You for all of the marvelous things You have done.

—Amen

HONESTY

The man of integrity walks securely, but he who takes crooked paths will be found out.

—Proverbs 10:9 NIV

A false balance is abomination to the LORD: but a just weight is his delight.

—Proverbs 11:1 KJV

Therefore, seeing we have this ministry, as we have received mercy, we faint not; but have renounced the hidden things of dishonesty, not walking in craftiness, nor handling the word of God deceitfully; but, by manifestation of the truth, commending ourselves to every man's conscience in the sight of God.

—II Corinthians 4:1-2 KJV

Buy the truth and do not sell it; get wisdom, discipline, and understanding.

—Proverbs 23:23 NIV

...and ye shall know the truth, and the truth shall make you free.

—John 8:32 KJV

From the time we are children, we are taught that honesty is the best policy. But, honesty is not just the *best* policy, it is also *God's* policy. If we are to be servants worthy of His holy blessings, we must remember that truth is not just the best way, it is God's way.

＞‣◦◦◦‣＜

Honesty has a beautiful and refreshing simplicity about it. No ulterior motives. No hidden meanings. As honesty and integrity characterize our lives, there will be no need to manipulate others.

—*Chuck Swindoll*

—A Prayer—

Lord, truth is Your commandment. You instruct me to seek truth and to live righteously. Help me, Lord, always to live according to Your commandments. Sometimes, Lord, speaking the truth can be difficult, but let me speak forthrightly. And let me walk righteously and courageously so that others might see Your Grace reflected in my words and my deeds.

—*Amen*

HONORING GOD

Honor the LORD with thy substance, and with the firstfruits of all thine increase so shall thy barns be filled with plenty....

—Proverbs 3:9-10 KJV

Call upon Me in the day of trouble; I shall rescue you, and you will honor Me.

—Psalm 50:15 NASB

Surely the righteous shall give thanks unto thy name: the upright shall dwell in thy presence.

—Psalm 140:13 KJV

The LORD is my strength and song, and He has become my salvation; He is my God, and I will praise Him....

—Exodus 15:2 NKJV

Bless the LORD, O my soul, and forget not all his benefits....

—Psalm 103:2 KJV

How should we honor God? With our prayers and our praise, with our words and our deeds, with trust in Him and with faith in His Son. And, after all the blessings that God has given us, how should we express our thankfulness? By placing Him where He belongs: at the very center of our lives.

⊱⊱⊶⊷⊰⊰

Preoccupy my thoughts with your praise beginning today.

—Joni Eareckson Tada

—A PRAYER—

I speak Your praise, O Lord. I praise You from the depths of my heart, and I give thanks for Your goodness, for Your mercy, and for Your Son Jesus. Let me honor You every day of my life through my words and my deeds. Let me honor You, Dear Lord, with all that I am.

—Amen

HOPE

The Lord is good to those whose hope is in him, to the one who seeks him; it is good to wait quietly for the salvation of the Lord.

—Lamentations 3:25-27 NIV

Be of good courage, and he shall strengthen your heart, all ye that hope in the Lord.

—Psalm 31:24 KJV

…Be not afraid, only believe.

—Mark 5:37 KJV

And when the woman saw that she was not hid, she came trembling, and falling down before him, she declared unto him before all the people for what cause she had touched him, and how she was healed immediately. And he said unto her, Daughter, be of good comfort: thy faith hath made thee whole; go in peace.

—Luke 8:47-48 KJV

Be still, and know that I am God….

—Psalm 46:10 KJV

This world can be a place of trials and tribulations, but as believers, we are secure. We need never lose hope because God has promised us peace, joy, and eternal life. So, let us face each day with hope in our hearts and trust in our God, remembering always that God keeps His promises. Always.

⊱─┄◈─◉─◈┄─⊰

Everything that is done in the world is done by hope.

—Martin Luther

—A Prayer—

Lord, when my path is steep and my heart is troubled, let me trust in You. When I lose faith in this world, let me never lose faith in You. Remind me, Lord, that in every situation and in every season of life, You will love me and protect me. And, with You as my protector, Lord, I need never lose hope because You remain sovereign today and forever.

—Amen

HUMILITY

For whosoever exalteth himself shall be abased; and he that humbleth himself shall be exalted.

—Luke 14:11 KJV

...humility comes before honor.

—Proverbs 15:33 NIV

Yea, all of you be subject one to another, and be clothed with humility: for God resisteth the proud, and giveth grace to the humble.

—I Peter 5:5 KJV

Though the Lord is great, he cares for the humble, but he keeps his distance from the proud.

—Psalm 138:6 NLT

I will boast only in the Lord....

—Psalm 34:2 NLT

Who are the greatest among us? Are they the proud and the powerful? Hardly. The greatest among us are the humble servants who care less for their own glory and more for God's glory. If we seek greatness in God's eyes, we must forever praise God's good works, not our own.

><+>•○•<+>•<

We can never have more of true faith than we have of true humility.

—Andrew Murray

—A Prayer—

Heavenly Father, Jesus clothed Himself with humility when He chose to leave heaven and come to earth to live and die for all creation. Lord, He is my Master and my example. Clothe me with humility, Lord, so that I might be more like Your Son.

—Amen

Jesus

The next day John seeth Jesus coming unto him, and saith, Behold the Lamb of God, which taketh away the sin of the world!

—John 1:29 KJV

Jesus saith unto him, I am the way, the truth, and the life: no man cometh unto the Father, but by me. If ye had known me, ye should have known my Father also: and from henceforth ye know him, and have seen him.

—John 14:6-7 KJV

For I am persuaded, that neither death, nor life, nor angels, nor principalities, nor powers, nor things present, nor things to come, nor height, nor depth, nor any other creature, shall be able to separate us from the love of God, which is in Christ Jesus our Lord.

—Romans 8:38-39 KJV

For the Son of man is come to save that which was lost.

—Matthew 18:11 KJV

The old familiar hymn begins, "What a friend we have in Jesus...." No truer words were ever penned. Jesus is the sovereign friend and ultimate savior of mankind. Christ showed enduring love for His believers by willingly sacrificing His own life so that we might have eternal life. Let us love Him, praise Him, and share His message of salvation with our neighbors and with the world.

❖

Jesus Christ is the first and last, author and finisher, beginning and end, alpha and omega, and by Him all other things hold together. He must be first or nothing. God never comes next!

—Vance Havner

—A Prayer—

Thank You, Lord, for Your Son Jesus, the Savior of my life. You loved this world so dearly, Lord, that You sent Your Son to die so that we, Your children, might have life eternal. Let the love of Jesus be reflected in my words, my thoughts, and my deeds. Let me always count Jesus as my dearest friend, and let me share His transforming message with a world in desperate need of His peace.

—Amen

++

JOY

++

These things have I spoken unto you, that my joy might remain in you, and that your joy might be full.

—John 15:11 KJV

Rejoice evermore. Pray without ceasing. In every thing give thanks: for this is the will of God in Christ Jesus concerning you.

—I Thessalonians 5:16-18 KJV

You will show me the way of life, granting me the joy of your presence and the pleasures of living with you forever.

—Psalm 16:11 NLT

Delight thyself also in the LORD; and he shall give thee the desires of thine heart.

—Psalm 37:4 KJV

Rejoice, and be exceeding glad: for great is your reward in heaven....

—Matthew 5:12 KJV

Christ made it clear to His followers: He intended that His joy would become their joy. And it still holds true today: Christ intends that His believers share His love with His joy in their hearts. Today, share the joy of Christ in your heart, share it freely, just as Christ freely shared His joy with you.

⇥—◆→—◯—◆—⇤

A life of intimacy with God is characterized by joy.

—Oswald Chambers

—A Prayer—

Lord, You have told me to give thanks always and to rejoice in Your marvelous creation. Let me be a joyful Christian, Lord, and let me focus on Your blessings and on Your Love. Help me to make this day and every day a cause for celebration as I share the Good News of Your Son Jesus.

—Amen

JUDGING OTHERS

Judge not, and ye shall not be judged: condemn not, and ye shall not be condemned: forgive, and ye shall be forgiven....

—*Luke 6:37 KJV*

Therefore no one is to act as your judge in regard to food or drink or in respect to a festival or a new moon or a Sabbath day....

—*Colossians 2:16 NASB*

Either how canst thou say to thy brother, Brother, let me pull out the mote that is in thine eye, when thou thyself beholdest not the beam that is in thine own eye? Thou hypocrite, cast out first the beam out of thine own eye, and then shalt thou see clearly to pull out the mote that is in thy brother's eye.

—*Luke 42:KJV*

Therefore judge nothing before the time, until the Lord come, who both will bring to light the hidden things of darkness, and will make manifest the counsels of the hearts: and then shall every man have praise of God.

—*I Corinthians 4:5 KJV*

We have all fallen short of God's commandments, and He has forgiven us. We, too, must forgive others. And we must refrain from judging them. As Christian believers, we are warned that to judge others is to invite fearful consequences: to the extent we judge others, so, too, will we be judged by God. Let us refrain, then, from judging our neighbors. Instead, let us forgive them in the same way that God has forgiven us.

❖

Only the truly forgiven are truly forgiving.

—*C. S. Lewis*

—A Prayer—

Dear Lord, sometimes I am quick to judge others. But, You have commanded me not to judge. Keep me mindful, Lord, that when I judge others, I am living outside of Your will for my life. You have forgiven me, Lord. Let me forgive others, let me love them, and let me help them…without judging them.

—*Amen*

KINDNESS

Be ye therefore merciful, as your Father also is merciful.

—Luke 6:36 KJV

A kind man benefits himself, but a cruel man brings trouble on himself.

—Proverbs 11:17 NIV

A gentle answer turns away wrath, but a harsh word stirs up anger.

—Proverbs 15:1 NIV

A new commandment I give unto you, That ye love one another; as I have loved you....

—John 13:34 KJV

...Verily I say unto you, Inasmuch as ye have done it unto one of the least of these my brethren, ye have done it unto me.

—Matthew 25:40 KJV

The words of *Matthew 25:40* remind us that when we extend the hand of kindness to a person in need, so have we extended ourselves to our Lord and Savior, Christ Jesus. Let us be imitators of Jesus, treating both friends and strangers with kindness and respect. Jesus expects no less, and He deserves no less.

><+>+O+<+I+<

Make it a rule, and pray to God to help you to keep it, never, if possible, to lie down at night without being able to say: "I have made one human being at least a little wiser, or a little happier, or at least a little better this day."

— *Charles Kingsley*

—A Prayer—

Slow me down, Lord, that I might see the needs of those around me. Today, help me to show mercy on those in need. Today, let me spread kind words of thanksgiving and celebration in honor of Your Son. Today, let forgiveness rule my heart. And every day, Lord, let my love for Christ be reflected through deeds of kindness for those who need the healing touch of the Master's hand.

—*Amen*

LAUGHTER

A cheerful heart is good medicine....

—*Proverbs 17:22 NIV*

There is a time for everything, and a season for every activity under heaven:...a time to weep and a time to laugh, a time to mourn and a time to dance.

—*Ecclesiastes 3:1,4 NIV*

Thou wilt show me the path of life: in thy presence is fulness of joy; at thy right hand there are pleasures for evermore.

—*Psalm 16:11 KJV*

This is the day which the Lord hath made; we will rejoice and be glad in it.

—*Psalm 118:24 KJV*

...let the hearts of those who seek the Lord rejoice.

—*I Chronicles 16: 10-11 NIV*

*I*t has been said, quite correctly, that laughter is God's medicine. Today, as you go about your daily activities, approach life with a smile and a chuckle. After all, God created laughter for a reason...and Father indeed knows best. So laugh!

><+>·O·<+>·<

It is often just as sacred to laugh as it is to pray.
—*Chuck Swindoll*

—A Prayer—

*L*ord, when I begin to take myself or my life too seriously, let me laugh. When I rush from place to place, slow me down, Lord, and let me laugh. Put a smile on my face, Dear Lord, and let me share that smile with all who cross my path...and let me laugh.

—*Amen*

LOVING GOD

Jesus replied, "'Love the Lord your God with all your heart and with all your soul and with all your mind.' This is the first and greatest commandment. And the second is like it: 'Love your neighbor as yourself.' All the Law and the Prophets hang on these two commandments."

—*Matthew 22:37-40 NIV*

For this is the love of God, that we keep his commandments....

—*I John 5:3 KJV*

He that loveth not, knoweth not God; for God is love.

—*I John 4:8 KJV*

I will thank you, Lord with all my heart; I will tell of all the marvelous things you have done. I will be filled with joy because of you. I will sing praises to your name, O Most High.

—*Psalm 9:1-2 NLT*

C. S. Lewis observed, "A man's spiritual health is exactly proportional to his love for God." If we are to enjoy the spiritual health that God intends for our lives, we must praise Him and Love Him. And, this is as it should be…after all, He first loved us.

><->-O-<->-<

Everything in your Christian life, everything about knowing Him and experiencing Him, everything about knowing His will, depends on the quality of your love relationship to God.

—*Henry Blackaby*

—A Prayer—

God, You are love. I love You because of Your great love for me. And, as I love You more, Lord, I am then able to love my family and friends more. Let me be Your loving servant, Heavenly Father, today and throughout eternity.

—*Amen*

LOVING OTHERS

But now faith, hope, love, abide these three; but the greatest of these is love.

—*1 Corinthians 13:13 NASB*

As the Father hath loved me, so have I loved you; continue ye in my love.

—*John 15:9 KJV*

Let love and faithfulness never leave you ...write them on the tablet of your heart.

—*Proverbs 3:3 NIV*

And this commandment have we from him, That he who loveth God love his brother also.

—*I John 4:21 KJV*

And the Lord make you to increase and abound in love one toward another, and toward all men....

—*I Thessalonians 3:12 KJV*

The familiar words of *1st Corinthians 13* remind us that love is God's commandment. Faith is important, of course. So too is hope. But love is more important still. Christ showed His love for us on the cross, and, as Christians, we are called upon to return Christ's love by sharing it. Today, let us spread Christ's love by word and by example. And the greatest of these, of course, is example.

›—‹•›—○—‹•›—‹

He who is filled with love is filled with God Himself.

—*St. Augustine*

—A Prayer—

Lord, You have given me the gift of eternal love; let me share that gift with the world. Help me, Lord, to show kindness to those who cross my path and let me show tenderness and unfailing love to my family and friends. Make me generous, Lord, with words of encouragement and praise. And, help me always to reflect the love that Christ Jesus gave me so that through me, others might find Him.

—*Amen*

MATURITY

But grow in the grace and knowledge of our Lord and Savior Jesus Christ.

—*2 Peter 3:18 NIV*

Consider it pure joy, my brothers, whenever you face trials of many kinds, because you know that the testing of your faith develops perseverance. Perseverance must finish its work so that you may be mature and complete, not lacking anything.

—*James 1:2-4 NIV*

I press on toward the goal to win the prize for which God has called me heavenward in Christ Jesus.

—*Philippians 3:14 NIV*

...let the wise listen and add to their learning, and let the discerning get guidance....

—*Proverbs 1:5 NIV*

For the LORD giveth wisdom: out of his mouth cometh knowledge and understanding.

—*Proverbs 2:6 KJV*

Norman Vincent Peale had the following advice for Christians of all ages: "Ask the God who made you to keep remaking you." When we cease to grow, either emotionally or spiritually, we do ourselves a profound disservice. Instead, we should continue to grow every day of our lives. We do so by studying God's Word and living in His will.

>─┼─◆>─○─<◆─┼─<

Being childlike is commendable. Being childish is unacceptable.

—Chuck Swindoll

—A Prayer—

Thank You, Lord, that I am not yet what I am to become. The Holy Scripture says that You are at work in my life, continuing to help me grow and to mature in the faith. Show me Your wisdom, Lord, and let me live according to Your Word and Your will.

—Amen

MIRACLES

And Jesus looking upon them saith, With men it is impossible, but not with God: for with God all things are possible.

—*Mark 10:27 KJV*

Let every soul be subject unto the higher powers. For there is no power but of God: the powers that be are ordained of God.

—*Romans 13:1 KJV*

Search for the Lord and for his strength, and keep on searching. Think of the wonderful works he has done, the miracles and the judgments he handed down.

—*Psalm 105: 4-5 NLT*

…Be strong and courageous. Do not be terrified; do not be discouraged, for the Lord your God will be with you wherever you go.

—*Joshua 1: 9-10 NIV*

Is anything too hard for the Lord?

—*Genesis 18:14 KJV*

Sometimes, because we are imperfect human beings with limited understanding and limited faith, we place limitations on God. But God's power has no limitations. God will work miracles in our lives *if* we trust Him with everything we have and everything we are. When we do, we will experience the miraculous results of His endless love and His awesome power.

><+>·O·<+><

Too many Christians live below the miracle level.
—*Vance Havner*

—A PRAYER—

Heavenly Father, Your infinite power is beyond human understanding. With You, Lord, nothing is impossible. Keep me always mindful of Your power. When I lose hope, give me faith; when others lose hope, let me tell them of Your glory and Your works. Today and every day, Lord, let me expect the miraculous, and let me trust in You.

—*Amen*

MISTAKES

Have mercy on me, O God, according to your unfailing love; according to your great compassion blot out my transgressions. Wash away all my iniquity and cleanse me from my sin.

—Psalm 51:1-2 NIV

If we confess our sins, he is faithful and just and will forgive us our sins and purify us from all unrighteousness.

—1 John 1:9 NIV

He who conceals his sins does not prosper, but whoever confesses and renounces them finds mercy.

—Proverbs 28:13 NIV

I waited patiently for the LORD; he turned to me and heard my cry. He lifted me out of the slimy pit, out of the mud and mire; he set my feet on a rock and gave me a firm place to stand. He put a new song in my mouth, a hymn of praise to our God....

—Psalm 40:1-3 NIV

The words are all too familiar and all too true: "To err is human…." Yes, we human beings are inclined to make mistakes, and lots of them. When we commit the inevitable blunders of life, let us be quick to correct our errors. And, when we are hurt by the mistakes of others, let us be quick to forgive, just as God has forgiven us.

><+>+O+<+><

Lord, when we are wrong, make us willing to change; and when we are right, make us easy to live with.

—*Peter Marshall*

—A Prayer—

Lord, I know that I am imperfect and that I fail You in many ways. Thank You for Your forgiveness and for Your unconditional love. Show me the error of my ways, Lord, that I might confess my wrongdoing and correct my mistakes. And, let me grow each day in wisdom and in faith.

—*Amen*

OBEDIENCE

It is the LORD your God you must follow, and him you must revere. Keep his commands and obey him; serve him and hold fast to him.

—*Deuteronomy 13:4 NIV*

Does the LORD delight in burnt offerings and sacrifices as much as in obeying the voice of the LORD? To obey is better than sacrifice....

—*1 Samuel 15:22 NIV*

For it is not those who hear the law who are righteous in God's sight, but it is those who obey the law who will be declared righteous.

—*Romans 2:13 NIV*

Jesus answered and said unto him, If a man love me, he will keep my words: and my Father will love him, and we will come unto him, and make our abode with him.

—*John 14:23 KJV*

The world and its desires pass away, but the man who does the will of God lives forever.

—*1 John 2:17 NIV*

*T*alking about God is easy; living by His commandments is considerably more difficult. But, unless we are willing to abide by God's laws, our righteous proclamations ring hollow. How can we best proclaim our love for the Lord? By obeying Him.

＞—◆>—○—<◆—◁

Let us remember therefore this lesson: That to worship our God sincerely we must evermore begin by hearkening to His voice, and by giving ear to what He commands us.

—John Calvin

—A Prayer—

*H*eavenly Father, when I turn my thoughts away from You and Your Word, I suffer. But when I obey Your commandments, when I place my faith in You, I am safe. Let me live according to Your commandments, Dear Lord. Direct my path far from the temptations and distractions of the world. And, let me discover Your will and follow it, this day and always.

—Amen

OPTIMISM

The Lord is my light and my salvation; whom shall I fear? The Lord is the strength of my life; of whom shall I be afraid?

—Psalm 27:1 KJV

Rejoice evermore. Pray without ceasing. In every thing give thanks: for this is the will of God in Christ Jesus concerning you.

—I Thessalonians 5:16-18 KJV

...let the hearts of those who seek the Lord rejoice. Look to the Lord and his strength; seek his face always.

—I Chronicles 16:10-11 NIV

Finally, brethren, whatsoever things are true, whatsoever things are honest, whatsoever things are just, whatsoever things are pure, whatsoever things are lovely, whatsoever things are of good report; if there be any virtue, and if there be any praise, think on these things.

—Philippians 4:8 KJV

As Christians, we have every reason to be optimistic about life. As John Calvin observed, "There is not one blade of grass, there is no color in this world that is not intended to make us rejoice." Today, think optimistically about yourself and your world. And, share your optimism with others. You'll be better for it…and so will they.

><+>—o—<+—<

At least ten times every day, affirm this thought: "I expect the best and, with God's help, will attain the best."

—*Norman Vincent Peale*

—A Prayer—

Lord, let me be an expectant Christian. Let me expect the best from You, and let me look for the best in others. If I become discouraged, Lord, turn my thoughts and my prayers to You. Let me trust You, Lord, to direct my life. And, let me be Your faithful, hopeful, optimistic servant every day that I live.

—*Amen*

PATIENCE

Be still before the Lord and wait patiently for him....

—*Psalm 37:7 NIV*

A man's wisdom gives him patience; it is to his glory to overlook an offense.

—*Proverbs 19:11 NIV*

For ye have need of patience, that, after ye have done the will of God, ye might receive the promise.

—*Hebrews 10:36 KJV*

...but we glory in tribulations also; knowing that tribulation worketh patience; and patience, experience; and experience, hope....

—*Romans 5:3-4 KJV*

We urge you, brethren, admonish the unruly, encourage the fainthearted, help the weak, be patient with everyone.

—*I Thessalonians 5:14 NASB*

*F*riendship requires patience. From time to time, even our most considerate friends may do things that worry us, confuse us, or anger us. Why do even the most loyal friends frustrate us on occasion? Because they are human. And, it is precisely because they are human that we must, from time to time, be patient with their shortcomings (as they, too, must be patient with ours). Today and every day, let us be understanding and patient with our friends. After all, think how patient God has been with us.

⊱┈◈┈○┈◈┈⊰

Patience is the companion of wisdom.

—*St. Augustine*

—A Prayer—

*D*ear Lord, let me live according to Your plan and according to Your timetable. When I am hurried, Lord, slow me down. When I become impatient with others, give me empathy. Today, Lord, let me be a patient Christian, and let me trust in You and in Your master plan.

—*Amen*

PEACE

And let the peace of God rule in your hearts...and be ye thankful.

—Colossians 3:15 KJV

Be perfect, be of good comfort, be of one mind, live in peace; and the God of love and peace shall be with you.

—II Corinthians 13:11 KJV

Return unto thy rest, O my soul; for the LORD hath dealt bountifully with thee.

—Psalm 116:7 KJV

Come to me all you who are weary and burdened, and I will give you rest. Take my yoke upon you and learn from me, for I am gentle and humble in heart, and you will find rest for your soul. For my yoke is easy and my burden is light.

—Matthew 11:28-30 NIV

Peace I leave with you, my peace I give unto you: not as the world giveth, give I unto you. Let not your heart be troubled, neither let it be afraid.

—John 14:27 KJV

The beautiful words of *John 14:27* give us hope: Jesus offers peace, not as the world gives, but as He alone gives. We, as believers, can accept His peace, and when we do, we are transformed. Today, let us claim the inner peace that is our spiritual birthright: the peace of Jesus Christ. It is offered freely; it has been paid for in full: it is ours for the asking. Let us accept His peace and then share it.

⊰•⊱•⊰•⊱

The peace that Jesus gives is never engineered by circumstances on the outside.

—*Oswald Chambers*

—A Prayer—

Lord, when I turn my thoughts and prayers to You, I feel the peace that You intend for my life. But sometimes I am distracted by the busyness of the day or the demands of the moment. When I am worried or anxious, Lord, turn my thoughts back to You. You are the Giver of all things good, Dear Lord, and You give me peace when I draw close to You. Help me to trust Your will, to follow Your commands, and to accept Your peace, today and forever.

—*Amen*

PERSEVERANCE

But the Lord is my defence; and my God is the rock of my refuge.

—Psalm 94:22 KJV

Cast thy burden upon the Lord, and he shall sustain thee; he shall never suffer the righteous to be moved.

—Psalm 55:22 KJV

...I do not consider myself yet to have taken hold of it. But one thing I do: Forgetting what is behind and straining toward what is ahead, I press on toward the goal to win the prize for which God has called me heavenward in Christ Jesus

—Philippians 3:13,14 NIV

For I the LORD thy God will hold thy right hand, saying unto thee, Fear not; I will help thee.

—Isaiah 41:13 KJV

God is our refuge and strength, a very present help in trouble.

—Psalm 46:1 KJV

The old saying is as true today as it was when it was first spoken: "Life is a marathon, not a sprint." Life, indeed, requires perseverance, so wise travelers select a traveling companion who never tires and never falters. That partner, of course, is God. Are you tired? Ask God for strength. Are you discouraged? Believe in His promises. Are you defeated? Pray as if everything depended upon God, and work as if everything depended upon youself. With God's help, you can persevere...and you will.

><+>+o+<+><

Keep adding, keep walking, keep advancing; do not stop, do not turn back, do not turn from the straight road.

—*St. Augustine*

—A Prayer—

Lord, sometimes, this life is difficult. Sometimes, we are burdened or fearful. Sometimes, we cry tears of bitterness or loss, but even then, You never leave our sides. Today, Lord, let me be a finisher of my faith. Let me persevere— even if the day is difficult—and let me follow Your Son Jesus Christ this day and forever.

—*Amen*

PRAISE

Sing praises to God, sing praises: sing praises unto our King, sing praises. For God is the King of all the earth: sing ye praises with understanding.

—Psalm 47:6-7 KJV

Praise ye the LORD. O give thanks unto the LORD; for he is good: for his mercy endureth for ever.

—Psalm 106:1 KJV

Rejoice evermore. Pray without ceasing. In every thing give thanks: for this is the will of God in Christ Jesus concerning you.

—I Thessalonians 5:16-18 KJV

It is good to give thanks to the Lord, to sing praises to the Most High. It is good to proclaim your unfailing love in the morning, your faithfulness in the evening.

—Psalm 92:2-3 NLT

When is the best time to praise God? In church? Before dinner is served? When we tuck little children into bed? None of the above. The best time to praise God is all day, every day, to the greatest extent we can, with thanksgiving in our hearts, and with a song on our lips. Today, may we find a little more time to lift our thankful hearts to God in prayer. And, may we praise Him for all that He has done. We owe God everything, including our praise.

›—•◆—○—◆•—‹

We should spend as much time in thanking God for his benefits as we do asking him for them.

—*St. Vincent de Paul*

—A Prayer—

Lord, Your hand created the smallest grain of sand and the grandest stars in the heavens. You watch over Your entire creation, and You watch over me. Thank You, Lord, for loving this world so much that You sent Your Son to die for our sins. Let me always be grateful for the priceless gift of Your Son, and let me praise Your holy name forever.

—*Amen*

PRAYER

The effective prayer of a righteous man can accomplish much.

—James 5:16 NASB

Ask, and it shall be given you; seek, and ye shall find; knock, and it shall be opened unto you: for every one that asketh receiveth; and he that seeketh findeth; and to him that knocketh it shall be opened.

—Matthew 7:7-8 KJV

Rejoice evermore. Pray without ceasing. In every thing give thanks: for this is the will of God in Christ Jesus concerning you.

—I Thessalonians 5:16-18 KJV

Watch ye therefore, and pray always, that ye may be accounted worthy to escape all these things that shall come to pass, and to stand before the Son of man.

—Luke 21:36 KJV

*P*rayer changes things *and* it changes us. Today, instead of turning things over in your mind, turn them over to God in prayer. Instead of worrying about your next decision, ask God to lead the way. Don't limit your prayers to meals or to bedtime. Pray constantly about things great and small. God is listening, and He wants to hear from you.

><+>-0-<+><

Get into the habit of dealing with God about everything.

—Oswald Chambers

—A Prayer—

I pray to You, my heavenly Father, because You desire it and because I need it. Prayer not only changes things, but, more importantly, it changes me. Help me, Lord, never to face the demands of the day without first spending time with You.

—Amen

RENEWAL

Create in me a clean heart, O God; and renew a right spirit within me.

—*Psalm 51:10 KJV*

I will give you a new heart and put a new spirit in you….

—*Ezekiel 36: 26 NIV*

…let the hearts of those who seek the Lord rejoice. Look to the Lord and his strength; seek his face always.

—*I Chronicles 16: 10-11 NIV*

For He has satisfied the thirsty soul, and the hungry soul He has filled with what is good.

—*Psalm 107:9 NASB*

Come unto me, all ye that labor and are heavy laden, and I will give you rest.

—*Matthew 11:28 KJV*

Even the most inspired Christians can, from time to time, find themselves running on empty. The demands of daily life can drain us of our strength and rob us of the joy that is rightfully ours in Christ. When we find ourselves tired, discouraged, or worse, there is a source from which we can draw the power needed to recharge our spiritual batteries. That source is God.

⇒⊹⋄⊹─○─⊹⋄⊹⇐

He is the God of wholeness and restoration.
—*Stormie Omartian*

—A PRAYER—

Heavenly Father, sometimes I am troubled, and sometimes I grow weary. When I am weak, Lord, give me strength. When I am discouraged, renew me. When I am fearful, let me feel Your healing touch. Let me always trust in Your promises, Lord, and let me draw strength from those promises and from Your unending love.

—*Amen*

REPENTANCE

Therefore this is what the Lord says: "If you repent, I will restore you that you may serve me...."

—*Jeremiah 15:19 NIV*

But their scribes and Pharisees murmured against his disciples, saying, Why do ye eat and drink with publicans and sinners? And Jesus answering said unto them, They that are whole need not a physician; but they that are sick. I came not to call the righteous, but sinners to repentance.

—*Luke 5:30-32 KJV*

But seek first his kingdom and his righteousness, and all these things will be given to you as well.

—*Matthew 6:33 NIV*

The steps of a good man are ordered by the LORD....

—*Psalm 37:23 KJV*

Who among us has sinned? All of us. But, God calls upon us to turn away from sin by following His commandments. And the good news is this: When we do ask God's forgiveness and turn our hearts to Him, He forgives us absolutely and completely.

❧———◦———❧

The bedrock of Christianity is repentance.
—*Oswald Chambers*

—A Prayer—

When I fail to follow Your commandments, Lord, I must not only confess my sins, I must also turn from them. When I fall short, help me to change. When I stray from You, guide me back to Your side. Forgive my sins, Dear Lord, and help me live from this day forward according to Your plan for my life.

—*Amen*

RIGHTEOUSNESS

Therefore, brethren, stand fast, and hold the traditions which ye have been taught, whether by word, or our epistle.

—*II Thessalonians 2:15 KJV*

Beloved, follow not that which is evil, but that which is good. He that doeth good is of God: but he that doeth evil hath not seen God.

—*III John 1:11 KJV*

For whosoever shall do the will of my Father which is in heaven, the same is my brother, and sister, and mother.

—*Matthew 12:50 KJV*

How blessed are those whose way is blameless, who walk in the law of the LORD. How blessed are those who observe his testimonies, who seek Him with all *their* heart.

—*Psalm 119: 1-2 NASB*

For thou, LORD, wilt bless the righteous....

—*Psalm 5:12 KJV*

*O*swald Chambers, author of the classic devotional text *My Utmost For His Highest*, advised, "Never support an experience which does not have God as its source, and faith in God as its result." These words serve as a powerful reminder that, as Christians, we are called to walk with God and to obey His commandments. We should always be examples of righteous living to our friends and neighbors. So, we can reap the blessings that God has promised to all those who live according to His will and His word.

>─◆─○─◆─<

We must appropriate the tender mercy of God every day after conversion or problems quickly develop. We need his grace daily in order to live a righteous life.

—Jim Cymbala

—A Prayer—

*L*ord, this world is filled with various temptations and distractions. When I turn my thoughts away from You and Your Word, Lord, I suffer. But when I trust in Your commandments, I am safe. Direct my path far from the temptations and distractions of the world. Let me discover Your will and follow it, Dear Lord, this day and always.

—Amen

SALVATION

Everyone who calls on the name of the Lord will be saved.

—*Romans 10:13 NIV*

I tell you the truth, he who believes has everlasting life.

—*John 6:47 NIV*

For it is by grace you have been saved, through faith—and this not from yourselves, it is the gift of God....

—*Ephesians 2:8 NIV*

For God sent not his Son into the world to condemn the world; but that the world through him might be saved.

—*John 3:17 KJV*

These things have I written unto you that believe on the name of the Son of God; that ye may know that ye have eternal life....

—*I John 5:13 KJV*

The familiar words of *Ephesians 2:8* make God's promise perfectly clear: *For it is by grace you have been saved, through faith....* We are saved not because of our good deeds but because of our faith in Christ. May we, who have been given so much, praise our Savior throughout eternity.

❧

Our salvation comes to us so easily because it cost God so much.

—*Oswald Chambers*

—A Prayer—

My salvation is in You, O Lord. My soul finds rest in You through Your Son Jesus Christ. The gift of salvation brings meaning to my life on earth and life eternal with You in heaven. Let me praise You and give thanks for Your glorious gift.

—*Amen*

SEEKING GOD

The LORD is with you when you are with him. If you seek him, he will be found by you....

—2 Chronicles 15:2 NIV

The LORD is good to those whose hope is in him, to the one who seeks Him....

—Lamentations 3:25 NIV

This is what the LORD says to the house of Israel: "Seek me and live...."

—Amos 5:4 NIV

But if from there you seek the LORD your God, you will find him if you look for him with all your heart and with all your soul.

—Deuteronomy 4:29 NIV

But seek first his kingdom and his righteousness, and all these things will be given to you as well.

—Matthew 6:33 NIV

*W*here is God? He is everywhere you have ever been and everywhere you will ever go. He is with you night and day; He knows your every thought; He hears every heartbeat. When you earnestly seek Him, you will find Him because He is here, waiting patiently for you to reach out to Him…right here.

><+>+O+<+><

Seeking after God is a two-pronged endeavor. It requires not only humility to say, "God, I need you," but also a heart that desires a pure life that is pleasing to the Lord.

—*Jim Cymbala*

—A Prayer—

*H*ow comforting it is, Lord, to know that if I seek You, I will find You. Let me reach out to You, Heavenly Father, and let me praise You for revealing Your Word, Your way, and Your love.

—*Amen*

SERVING GOD

No servant can serve two masters. Either he will hate the one and love the other, or he will be devoted to the one and despise the other. You cannot serve both God and Money.

—Luke 16:13 NIV

Jesus said to him, "Away from me, Satan! For it is written: 'Worship the Lord your God, and serve him only.'"

—Matthew 4:10 NIV

So then, men ought to regard us as servants of Christ and as those entrusted with the secret things of God. Now it is required that those who have been given a trust must prove faithful.

—1 Corinthians 4:1,2 NIV

Store up for yourselves treasures in heaven, where moth and rust do not destroy, and where thieves do not break in and steal. For where your treasure is there your heart will be also.

—Matthew 6:20,21 NIV

When Jesus was tempted by Satan, the Master's response was unambiguous. Jesus chose to worship the Lord *and serve him only.* We, as followers of Christ, must follow in His footsteps. When we place God in a position of secondary importance, we do ourselves great harm. But, when we imitate Jesus and place the Lord in His rightful place—at the center of our lives—then we claim spiritual treasures that will endure forever.

>-+--0-+-<

God wants us to serve Him with a willing spirit, one that would choose no other way.

—*Beth Moore*

—A Prayer—

Dear Lord, sometimes I am distracted by the busyness and confusion of daily life. But, if I stray from You, Lord, I suffer. Let me serve You first, Lord, and let me place my devotion to You above every other aspect of my life. And, then, with Your love dwelling in my heart, let me share Your love with family, and friends, and all who cross my path.

—*Amen*

SERVING OTHERS

And he sat down, and called the twelve, and saith unto them, If any man desire to be first, the same shall be last of all, and servant of all.

—Mark 9:35 KJV

Neither be ye called masters: for one is your Master, even Christ. But he that is greatest among you shall be your servant.

—Matthew 23:10-11 KJV

Even so faith, if it hath not works, is dead, being alone.

—James 2:17 KJV

Therefore, since we receive a kingdom which cannot be shaken, let us show gratitude by which we may offer to God an acceptable service with reverence and awe;

—Hebrews 12:28 NASB

Therefore all things whatsoever ye would that men should do to you, do ye even so to them: for this is the law and the prophets.

—Matthew 7:12 KJV

The teachings of Jesus are crystal clear: We achieve greatness through service to others. But, as weak human beings, we sometimes fall short as we seek to puff ourselves up and glorify our own accomplishments. Jesus commands otherwise. If we seek spiritual greatness, we must first become servants.

><+>+O+<+><

In God's family, there is to be one great body of people: servants. In fact, that's the way to the top in his kingdom.

—*Chuck Swindoll*

—A Prayer—

Father in heaven…when Jesus humbled Himself and became a servant, He also became an example for His followers. Today, as I serve my family and friends, I do so in the name of Jesus, my Lord and Master.

—*Amen*

SHARING

In everything I did, I showed you that by this kind of hard work we must help the weak, remembering the words the Lord Jesus himself said: "It is more blessed to give than to receive."

—*Acts 20:35 NIV*

He that hath two coats, let him impart to him that hath none; and he that hath meat, let him do likewise.

—*Luke 3:11 KJV*

...the righteous give without sparing.

—*Proverbs 21:26 NIV*

You are the light of the world. A city on a hill cannot be hidden. Neither do people light a lamp and put it under a bowl. Instead they put it on its stand, and it gives light to everyone in the house. In the same way, let your light shine before men, that they may see your good deeds and praise your Father in heaven.

—*Matthew 5:14-16 NIV*

We live in a fast-paced, competitive world where it is easy to say, "Me first." But, God instructs us to do otherwise. In God's kingdom, those who proclaim, "Me first," are last. God loves a cheerful, selfless giver. If you seek greatness in God's eyes, look your neighbor squarely in the eye and say, "You first." When you do, you'll give glory to the humble servant who died for your sins: your Savior, Christ Jesus.

>─+◆+─O─+◆+─<

Since you cannot do good to all, you are to pay special regard to those who, by the accidents of time, or place, or circumstances, are brought into closer connection with you.

—St. Augustine

—A PRAYER—

Lord, I know there is no happiness in keeping Your blessings for myself. True joy is found in sharing what I have with others. Make me a generous, loving, humble servant, Dear Lord, as I follow the example of Your Son Jesus.

—Amen

SPEECH

A word aptly spoken is like apples of gold in settings of silver.

—Proverbs 25:11 NIV

May the words of my mouth and the meditation of my heart be pleasing in your sight, O LORD, my Rock and my Redeemer.

—Psalm 19:14 NIV

A wise man's heart guides his mouth, and his lips promote instruction.

—Proverbs 16:23 NIV

For out of the overflow of the heart the mouth speaks.

—Matthew 12:34 NIV

Do not let any unwholesome talk come out of your mouths, but only what is helpful for building others up according to their needs, that it may benefit those who listen.

—Ephesians 4:29 NIV

*T*hink before you speak: How wise is the man or woman who can communicate in this fashion. But all too often we speak first and think second…with unfortunate results. Today, seek to encourage all who cross your path. Measure your words carefully. Speak wisely, not impulsively. Your words will bring healing and comfort to a world that needs both.

><+>-o-<+-<

Words. Do you fully understand their power? Can any of us really grasp the mighty force behind the things we say? Do we stop and think before we speak, considering the potency of the words we utter?

—*Joni Eareckson Tada*

—A Prayer—

*L*ord, You have warned me that I will be judged by the words I speak. And, You have commanded me to choose my words carefully so that I might be a source of encouragement and hope to all whom I meet. Keep me mindful, Lord, that I have influence on many people…make me an influence for good. And may the words that I speak today be worthy of the One who has saved me forever.

—*Amen*

Strength

But the Lord is my defence; and my God is the rock of my refuge.

—*Psalm 94:22 KJV*

Cast thy burden upon the Lord, and he shall sustain thee; he shall never suffer the righteous to be moved.

—*Psalm 55:22 KJV*

...I do not consider myself yet to have taken hold of it. But one thing I do: Forgetting what is behind and straining toward what is ahead, I press on toward the goal to win the prize for which God has called me heavenward in Christ Jesus.

—*Philippians 3:13,14 NIV*

For I the LORD thy God will hold thy right hand, saying unto thee, Fear not; I will help thee.

—*Isaiah 41:13 KJV*

God is our refuge and strength, a very present help in trouble.

—*Psalm 46:1 KJV*

God is a never-ending source of strength and courage for those who call upon Him. In difficult times, God is there. When we see no hope, God reminds us of His promises. When we grieve, God wipes away our tears. Whatever our circumstances, God will protect us and care for us...if we let Him.

><+>+O+<+><

He stands fast as your rock, steadfast as your safeguard, sleepless as your watcher, valiant as your champion.

—*C. H. Spurgeon*

—A Prayer—

Lord, sometimes life is difficult. Sometimes, I am worried, weary, or heartbroken. But, when I lift my eyes to You, Lord, You strengthen me. When I am weak, You lift me up. Today, let me turn to You, Lord, for my strength and my salvation.

—*Amen*

TEMPTATION

No temptation has seized you except what is common to man. And God is faithful; he will not let you be tempted beyond what you can bear. But when you are tempted, he will also provide a way out so that you can stand up under it.

—I Corinthians 10:13 NIV

…be vigilant; because your adversary the devil, as a roaring lion, walketh about, seeking whom he may devour.

—I Peter 5:8 KJV

For we do not have a high priest who is unable to sympathize with our weaknesses, but we have one who has been tempted in every way, just as we are—yet was without sin.

—Hebrews 4:15 NIV

Blessed is the man that endureth temptation: for when he is tried, he shall receive the crown of life….

—James 1:12 KJV

How easy it is to be tempted in this crazy world. The devil, it seems, is working overtime these days, and causing pain and heartache in more places and in more ways than ever before. We, as Christians, must remain vigilant. Not only must we resist Satan when he confronts us, but we must also avoid those places where Satan can most easily tempt us. And, we must beware, and we must earnestly wrap ourselves in the protection of God's Holy Word. When we do, we are secure.

⊱⊰⋅⊰⋅⊙⋅⊱⋅⊱⊰

Ask Christ to come into your heart to forgive you and help you. When you do, Christ will take up residence in your life by His Holy Spirit, and when you face temptations and trials you will no longer face them alone.

—Billy Graham

—A Prayer—

Lord, life is filled with temptations to stray from Your chosen path. But, I face no temptation that You have not already met and conquered through my Lord and Savior Jesus Christ. He has been victorious over the devil's temptations, and He empowers me with the same strength to overcome.

—Amen

TESTIMONY

Also I say unto you, Whosoever shall confess me before men, him shall the Son of man also confess before the angels of God: but he that denieth me before men shall be denied before the angels of God.

—*Luke 12:8-9 KJV*

In your hearts set apart Christ as Lord. Always be prepared to give an answer to everyone who asks you to give the reason for the hope that you have.

—*I Peter 3:15 NIV*

And the night following, the Lord stood by him, and said, be of good cheer, Paul: for…thou hast testified of me….

—*Acts 23:11 KJV*

Whoever acknowledges me before men, I will also acknowledge him before my Father in heaven.

—*Matthew: 10:32 NIV*

*I*n his second letter to Timothy, Paul shares a message to believers of every generation when he writes, "God has not given us a spirit of timidity." Paul's meaning is clear: When sharing our testimonies, we, as Christians, must be courageous, forthright, and unashamed.

━━◆◇◆━━

I look upon all the world as my parish.

—*John Wesley*

—A PRAYER—

*D*ear Lord, You sent Your Son Jesus to die on a cross for me. Jesus endured indignity, suffering, and death so that I might live. Because He lives, I, too, have Your promise of eternal life. Let me share this good news, Lord, with a world that so desperately needs Your healing hand and the salvation of Your Son. Today, let me share the message of Jesus Christ through my words and my deeds.

—*Amen*

THANKSGIVING

And let the peace of God rule in your hearts...and be ye thankful.

—Colossians 3:15 KJV

In everything give thanks; for this is God's will for you in Christ Jesus.

—I Thessalonians 5:18 NIV

Make a joyful noise unto the Lord all ye lands. Serve the lord with gladness: come before his presence with singing. Know ye that the Lord he is God: it is he that hath made us, and not we ourselves; we are his people and the sheep of his pasture. Enter into his gates with thanksgiving, and into his courts with praise; be thankful unto him and bless his name. For the Lord is good; his mercy is everlasting; and his truth endureth to all generations.

—Psalm 100:1-5 KJV

I will praise the name of God with a song, and will magnify him with thanksgiving.

—Psalm 69:30 KJV

As believing Christians, we are blessed beyond measure. Thanksgiving should become a habit, a regular part of our daily routines. Yes, God has blessed us beyond measure, and we owe Him everything, including our eternal praise. To paraphrase the familiar children's blessing, "God is great, God is good, let us thank Him for…everything!"

━━◆◆◇◆◆━━

Why wait until the fourth Thursday in November? Thanksgiving to God should be an everyday affair. The time to be thankful is now.

—*Jim Gallery*

—A Prayer—

Dear Jesus, I know that You are the bread of life and the Savior of my life. When I am weak, You give me strength, and when I am worried, You give me peace. Thank You, Lord, for the gift of eternal life and for the gift of eternal love. May I be ever grateful, and may I share Your good news with a world that so desperately needs Your healing grace.

—*Amen*

TODAY

This is the day the Lord has made; let us rejoice and be glad in it.

—*Psalm 118:24 NIV*

For he says, "In the time of my favor I heard you, and in the day of salvation I helped you." I tell you, now is the time of God's favor, now is the day of salvation.

—*II Corinthians 6:2 NIV*

…encourage one another daily, as long as it is Today….

—*Hebrews 3:13 NIV*

The heavens declare the glory of God; and the firmament showeth his handiwork.

—*Psalm 19:1 KJV*

I know whom I have believed, and am convinced that he is able to guard what I have entrusted to him for that day.

—*II Timothy 1:12 NIV*

For Christian believers, every day begins and ends with God and His Son. Christ came to this earth to give us abundant life and eternal salvation. Our task is to accept Christ's grace with joy in our hearts and praise on our lips. So, treasure this day; it is a gift from God. God's love for you is infinite. Accept it joyously and be thankful.

>—◆—○—◆—<

Love, joy, peace, patience, kindness, goodness, faithfulness, gentleness, and self-control. To these I commit my day. If I succeed, I will give thanks. If I fail, I will seek his grace. And then when this day is done, I will place my head on my pillow and rest.

—Max Lucado

—A Prayer—

Help me, Father, to learn from the past but not live in it. And, help me to plan for the future but not to worry about it. This is the day You have given me, Lord. Let me use it according to Your master plan, and let me give thanks for Your blessings. Enable me to live each moment to the fullest, totally involved in Your will.

—Amen

TRUST IN GOD

Let not your heart be troubled: ye believe in God, believe also in me.

—John 14:1 KJV

So do not worry, saying "What shall we eat?" or "What shall we drink?" or "What shall we wear?" For the Pagans run after all these things, and your heavenly father knows that you need them. But seek first his kingdom and his righteousness, and all these things will be given to you as well. Therefore do not worry about tomorrow, for tomorrow will worry about itself. Each day has enough trouble of its own.

—Matthew 6:31-34 NIV

But it is good for me to draw near to God: I have put my trust in the Lord GOD....

—Psalm 73:28 KJV

Trust in the LORD with all thine heart; and lean not unto thine own understanding. In all thy ways acknowledge him, and he shall direct thy paths.

—Proverbs 3:5-6 KJV

*D*o you aspire to do great things for God's kingdom? Then trust Him. Trust Him with every aspect of your life. Trust Him with your relationships. Trust Him with your finances. Follow His commandments and pray for His guidance. Then, wait patiently for God's revelations and for His blessings. In His own fashion and in His own time, God will bless you in ways that you never could have imagined.

><+>—0—<+><

Trust the past to God's mercy, the present to God's love and the future to God's providence.

—*St. Augustine*

—A PRAYER—

*L*ord, when I trust in things of this earth, I will be disappointed. But, when I put my faith in You, I am secure. You are my rock and my shield. Upon Your firm foundation I will build my life. When I am worried, Lord, let me trust in You. You will love me and protect me, and You will share Your boundless grace today, tomorrow, and forever.

—*Amen*

TRUTH

For there is nothing covered, that shall not be revealed; neither hid, that shall not be known. Therefore, whatsoever ye have spoken in darkness shall be heard in the light; and that which ye have spoken in the ear in closets shall be proclaimed upon the housetops.

—Luke 12:1-3 KJV

Therefore laying aside falsehood, speak truth each one of you with his neighbor, for we are members of one another.

—Ephesians 4:25 NASB

Buy the truth and do not sell it; get wisdom, discipline, and understanding.

—Proverbs 23:23 NIV

And ye shall know the truth, and the truth shall make you free.

—John 8:32 KJV

The words of *John 8:32* are both familiar and profound: *ye shall know the truth, and the truth shall make you free.* Truth is God's way: He commands His children to live in truth, and He rewards those who follow His commandment. Jesus is the personification of a perfect, liberating truth that offers salvation to mankind. Do you seek to walk with God? Then you must walk in truth, and you must walk with the Savior.

><+>–0–<+>–<

Those who walk in truth walk in liberty.

—*Beth Moore*

—A Prayer—

Dear Lord, You command Your children to walk in truth. Let me follow Your commandment. Sometimes, Lord, when it is difficult to speak truthfully, give me the courage to speak honestly. And, let me walk righteously with You so that others might see Your eternal truth reflected in my words and my deeds.

—*Amen*

WISDOM

For the LORD giveth wisdom: out of his mouth cometh knowledge and understanding.

—Proverbs 2:6 KJV

...the wisdom that is from above is first pure, then peaceable, gentle, and easy to be entreated, full of mercy and good fruits, without partiality, and without hypocrisy.

—James 3:17 KJV

Reverence for the Lord is the foundation of true wisdom. The rewards of wisdom come to all who obey him.

—Psalm 111:10 NLT

Let the word of Christ dwell in you richly in all wisdom; teaching and admonishing one another in psalms and hymns and spiritual songs, singing with grace in your hearts to the Lord.

—Colossians 3:16 KJV

*W*isdom is like a savings account: If you add to it consistently, then eventually you'll have a great sum. The secret to success is consistency. Do you seek wisdom? Then seek it every day, and seek it in the right place. That place, of course, is God's Holy Word.

⋗⊶⊙⊷⊰

Don't expect wisdom to come into your life like great chunks of rock on a conveyor belt. Wisdom comes privately from God as a byproduct of right decisions, godly reactions, and the application of spiritual principles to daily circumstances.

—*Chuck Swindoll*

—A Prayer—

I seek wisdom, Lord, not as the world gives, but as You give. Lead me in Your ways and teach me from Your word so that, in time, my wisdom might glorify Your kingdom, Lord, and Your Son.

—*Amen*

WORK

But let every man prove his own work, and then shall he have rejoicing in himself alone, and not in another. For every man shall bear his own burden.

—Galatians 6:4-5 KJV

But this I say, He which soweth sparingly shall reap also sparingly; and he which soweth bountifully shall reap also bountifully.

—II Corinthians 9:6 KJV

The plans of the diligent lead to profit as surely as haste leads to poverty.

—Proverbs 21:5 NIV

Be kindly affectioned one to another with brotherly love; in honor preferring one another; not slothful in business; fervent in spirit; serving the Lord; rejoicing in hope; patient in tribulation; continuing instant in prayer....

—Romans 12:10-12 KJV

$\mathcal{I}$t has been said that there are no short-cuts to anyplace worth going to. Hard work is not simply a proven way to get ahead, it's also part of God's plan for His children. God did not create us for lives of mediocrity; He created us for far greater things. Earning great things usually requires work and lots of it, which is perfectly fine with God. After all, He knows that we're up to the task, and He has big plans for us. Very big plans...

><+><><+><

We trust as if it all depended on God, and work as if it all depended on us.

—*C. H. Spurgeon*

—A Prayer—

$\mathcal{L}$ord, I know that You desire a bountiful harvest for all Your children. But, You have instructed us that we must sow before we reap, not after. Help me, Lord, to sow the seeds of Your abundance everywhere I go. Let me be diligent in all my undertakings and give me patience to wait for Your harvest. In time, Lord, let me reap the harvest that is found in Your will for my life.

—*Amen*

WORRY

Therefore I tell you, do not worry about your life, what you will eat or drink; or about your body, what you will wear. Is life not more important than food and the body more important than clothes? Look at the birds of the air; they do not sow or reap or store away in barns, and yet your heavenly father feeds them. Are you not much more valuable than they? Who of you by worrying can add a single hour to his life.

—*Matthew 6: 25-27 NIV*

God is our refuge and strength, a very present help in trouble.

—*Psalm 46:1 KJV*

It is better to trust in the LORD than to put confidence in man. It is better to trust in the LORD than to put confidence in princes.

—*Psalm 118:8-9 KJV*

I will lift up mine eyes unto the hills, from whence cometh my help. My help cometh from the Lord, which made heaven and earth.

—*Psalm 121: 1-2 KJV*

*A*re you worried? Take your worries to God. Are you troubled? Take your troubles to Him. Does your world seem to be trembling beneath your feet? Seek protection from the One who cannot be moved. The same God who created the universe will protect you if you ask Him...so ask Him.

><+<>+<O+<+><

The beginning of anxiety is the end of faith, and the beginning of true faith is the end of anxiety.

—George Mueller

—A Prayer—

*L*ord, You sent Your Son to live as a man on this earth, and You know what it means to be completely human. You understand my worries and fears, Lord, and You forgive me when I am weak. When my faith begins to wane, Help me, Lord, to trust You more. And, with Your Holy Word on my lips and with the love of Your Son in my heart, let me live courageously, faithfully, prayerfully, and thankfully today and every day.

—Amen

WORSHIP

I was glad when they said unto me, Let us go into the house of the LORD.

—Psalm 122:1 KJV

Then saith Jesus unto him, Get thee hence, Satan: for it is written, Thou shalt worship the Lord thy God, and him only shalt thou serve.

—Matthew 4:10 KJV

But the hour cometh, and now is, when the true worshippers shall worship the Father in spirit and in truth: for the Father seeketh such to worship him.

—John 4:23 KJV

O come, let us sing unto the LORD: let us make a joyful noise to the rock of our salvation. Let us come before his presence with thanksgiving, and make a joyful noise unto him with psalms.

—Psalm 95:1-2 KJV

If any man thirst, let him come unto me, and drink.

—John 7:37 KJV

When we worship God, either alone or in the company of fellow believers, we are blessed. When we fail to worship God, for whatever reason, we forfeit the spiritual riches that are rightfully ours. Every day provides opportunities to put God where He belongs: at the center of our lives. Let us worship Him, and only Him, today and always.

><+>+O+<+<

Don't ever come to church without coming as though it were the first time, as though it could be the best time, and as though it might be the last time.

—Vance Havner

—A Prayer—

Heavenly Father, this world can be a place of distractions and temptations. But when I worship You, Lord, You direct my path and You cleanse my heart. Let today and every day be a time of worship and praise. Let me worship You in everything that I think and do. Thank You, Lord for the priceless gift of Your Son Jesus. Let me be worthy of that gift, and let me give You the praise and the glory forever.

—Amen